# Advent Week 1 Devotion – Hope

**SAY:** Advent is a season of waiting. In winter, the earth tilts away from the sun. In the northern hemisphere, the season of Advent includes the longest night of the year or the winter solstice. As the nights get longer, we wait for the joy of Jesus' birth. We read stories from the Bible to help fill us with hope and remember God's love.

**READ** Psalm 122 together from a CEB kids' Bible or online Bible source.

**SAY:** Today's reading is a song. We sing songs to help us remember God's promises. Songs fill us with hope during the Advent season.

**ASK:** Do you have a favorite Christmas song?

**PRAY:** God of hope, thank you for all the reasons we look forward to the Christmas season. We are looking forward to (invite everyone to list things you are looking forward to doing during Advent). We love you. Amen.

## Family Activity Options

- Sing a favorite Christmas carol together.
- Practice patience while playing a favorite board game together.
- Print the Advent Wreath found by using the QR code in the front of the book and create your candles. You will also find directions to create your own flame-free Advent candles.
- Light your first candle this week using your flame-free candles or a battery-operated tealight.

# Advent Week 2 Devotion – Peace

**SAY:** Advent helps us know more about God. God cares for us and helps us feel peace, even through hard times.

**READ** Matthew 3:1-12 together from a CEB kids' Bible or online Bible source.

**SAY:** Today's reading is about Jesus' cousin, John! John helped people connect to God, despite hard things happening in the world. John told people that one day, Jesus would turn people toward God and people would know peace.

**ASK:** How can you show God's love to others this Advent?

**PRAY:** God of peace, we thank you for your promises. Help us share your peace with everyone we meet. Amen.

## Family Activity Options

- Pick a nonprofit organization to donate money or time together.
- Create a peaceful corner with soft blankets, pillows, and seating. Spend time in your peaceful corner during the busy holiday season.
- Write a prayer together to pray when you wake up in the morning that reminds you of God's peace and love.
- Light your second candle together this week using your flame-free candles or a battery-operated tealight.

©2025 Cokesbury
ART: Adobe Stock

# Kids' Advent Calendar of Devotions

## Table of Contents

About This Resource . . . . . . . . . . 2

Family Devotions . . . . . . . . . . 3–6

Christ Ornaments . . . . . . . . . . . . 7

Advent Word Search . . . . . . . . . 8

Names for Jesus . . . . . . . . . . . . . 9

An Advent Sanctuary . . . . . . . . . 10

The Road to Bethlehem . . . . . . . 11

Family Activity Calendar . . . . . 12–13

The Shepherds' Journey . . . . . . . 14

Christmas Jokes . . . . . . . . . . . . 15

Christmas Comic Strip . . . . . . 16–17

Homemade Hot Cocoa . . . . . . . . 18

Ornament Connect-the-Dots . . . . 19

Spot the Differences . . . . . . . . . 20

Mindful Coloring . . . . . . . . . . . 21

Prayers for Advent . . . . . . . . . . . 22

Advent Prayer Journal . . . . . . . . 23

Finger Prayer Labyrinth . . . . . . . 24

### EDITORIAL / DESIGN TEAM

Megan Teegarden-Ranjit . . . Team Lead/Editor
Sarah Gregory . . . . . . . . . . . Associate Editor
Norma Bates . . . . . . . . . . . . . . . . Copyeditor
Matt Allison . . . . Production & Design Manager

### ADMINISTRATIVE TEAM

Rev. Brian K. Milford . . . President and Publisher
Marjorie M. Pon . Associate Publisher and Editor
of Church School Publications

Copyright © 2025 by Abingdon Press
All rights reserved.

No part of this work may be reproduced or transmitted in any form or by any means, electronic or mechanical, including photocopying and recording, or by any information storage or retrieval system, except as may be expressly permitted by the 1976 Copyright Act, the 1998 Digital Millennium Copyright Act, or in writing from the publisher. Requests for permission can be addressed to Rights and Permissions, The United Methodist Publishing House, 810 12th Avenue South, Nashville, TN 37203-4704 or emailed to permissions@abingdonpress.com.

9781791040048 (Pack of 10)

Scripture quotations are taken from the Common English Bible, copyright 2011. Used by permission. All rights reserved.

MANUFACTURED IN THE UNITED STATES OF AMERICA

## About this Resource

Dear Parents and Caregivers,

The Kids' Advent Calendar of Devotions is designed to help the children in your life experience the wonder of Advent. In this book you will find many ways to engage in Advent discussions and activities as a family, as well as fun activities for your kids to do independently or together with you. This book was made with you and your family in mind! We hope that you find hope, joy, love, and peace within these pages as you explore the season of Advent.

The Cokesbury Kids Team

### Ways to Engage with this Resource:

- Set aside time each week to read the weekly Advent Devotions as a family.
- Tear out the Advent Calendar found in the center of this book and post it somewhere your family will see it each day. Do as many activities that work for you!
- Let your kids take this book to worship each Sunday during Advent. Pull it out during the sermon for quiet, engaging activities.
- Encourage your kids to bring this book with them anywhere else they might have down time.
- Let your children share what they are learning in this book over a meal.

### For even more fun, Advent content, scan the QR code below!

https://www.cokesburykids.com/kids-devotions-extras

© 2025 Cokesbury

# Advent Week 3 Devotion – Joy

**SAY:** Waiting for something new can be hard. But as we wait for Christmas, we are also full of joy! Look around at all the fun ways people prepare for Christmas.

**READ** Luke 1:46b-55 together from a CEB kids' Bible or online Bible source.

**SAY:** Today's reading is Mary's song. She sang it when she found out she would be Jesus' mother! Mary was filled with joy.

**ASK:** How do you like to show joy? What makes you joyful during Advent?

**PRAY:** God of joy, we come to you with excitement. Help us share our joy with others. Amen.

## Family Activity Options

- Plan a time to sing at your local nursing home or in your neighborhood.
- Clean out toys or clothing that you no longer use and donate the items.
- Have a Christmas music dance party! Move your body and share your joy.
- Light your third candle together this week using your flame-free candles or a battery-operated tealight.

# Advent Week 4 Devotion – Love

**SAY:** God's love is the most important part of the story of Advent. God sent Jesus to teach us how to love each other. We can share God's love every single day.

**READ** Matthew 1:18-25 together from a CEB kids' Bible or online Bible source.

**SAY:** Today's reading is about Jesus's earthly dad, Joseph. Joseph decided to raise Jesus as his own son after a visit from an angel! Joseph loved Jesus and cared for him as he grew up.

**ASK:** How do people show you love? How do you show love to others?

**PRAY:** God of love, thank you for your loving care. We pray especially for the people and things we love (invite everyone to list people and things they love). Help us spread love to others. Amen.

## Family Activity Options

- Create a love paper chain. Cut strips of paper, write the names of loved ones on each chain. Next, use a stapler to create interlocking rings. Use the chain to pray for loved ones each day until Christmas.
- Take turns sharing one thing you love about each person in your household.
- Pick a favorite Christmas movie and look for examples of love throughout the movie.
- Light your fourth candle together this week using your flame-free candles or a battery-operated tealight. On Christmas Eve or Christmas Day, light the middle Christ candle.
- Scan the QR code in the front of this book for a bonus Christmas Day devotional.

# Christ Ornaments

Christ ornaments are special ornaments that some people use to decorate their trees during Advent. Color the ornaments below with gold crayons. Scan the QR code in the front of this book to learn more about Christ ornaments.

# Advent Word Search

Find and circle the words that you may hear during Advent.

| C | Q | U | P | D | Y | G | V | X | J |
|---|---|---|---|---|---|---|---|---|---|
| W | A | D | V | E | N | T | S | F | O |
| H | X | N | A | I | A | F | Z | B | S |
| R | J | Q | E | B | W | C | D | G | E |
| V | E | O | Z | V | A | H | E | O | P |
| C | S | A | Y | L | I | N | P | Q | H |
| M | U | K | K | Y | T | U | L | S | M |
| E | S | P | J | W | I | H | O | P | E |
| M | A | R | Y | F | N | T | V | J | M |
| L | G | U | H | T | G | S | E | Z | I |

- ☐ ADVENT
- ☐ HOPE
- ☐ JESUS
- ☐ JOSEPH
- ☐ JOY
- ☐ LOVE
- ☐ MARY
- ☐ PEACE
- ☐ WAITING

# Names for Jesus

Jesus is called many other names in the Bible. Unscramble the words from Isaiah 9:6 to find out what they are.

Peace   Counselor   Father
Wonderful   Eternal   of
Mighty   God   Prince

ednWlrouf   runlosCeo   _____   _____

hiMygt   odG   _____   _____

nelratE   hFtrae   _____   _____

cenrPi   fo   eePca   _____   _____   _____

Which name do you like the most?

# An Advent Sanctuary

Advent is a special time where many people decorate their homes and churches. Color the Advent decorations to complete the picture below.

**What decorations does your home or church have for Advent?**

# The Road to Bethlehem

Complete Mary and Joseph's journey from Nazareth to Bethlehem, where Jesus was born.

**Nazareth**

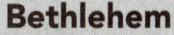

# Family Activity Calendar

| 30 DEVO | 1 Make the hot cocoa recipe on p. 18. | 2 Play with a Nativity set or make your own. | 3 Draw pictu piece own p |
|---|---|---|---|
| 7 DEVO | 8 Collect food to donate to a local food bank. | 9 | 10 Practi from p |
| 14 DEVO | 15 Pretend to be the magi. Start looking for Jesus everywhere you go! | 16 Make your own Christmas cards to mail to a friend. | 17 See p. Tell ea your fa jokes |
| 21 DEVO | 22 Write a thank-you note to someone who cares for your community. | 23 Look for Christmas lights around town. | 24 **Chris** Sing S togeth |
| 28 | 29 | 30 | 31 |

© 2025 Cokesbury
ART: Naoko Matsunaga/Illustration Online LLC

| | **4** Read Isaiah 51:1 together. | **5** Sing a favorite Christmas carol. | **6** Give someone a compliment. |
|---|---|---|---|
| | **11** Tell your favorite stuffed animal the story of Christmas. | **12** Tell someone you love them. | **13** Practice a new kind of prayer using the labyrinth on p. 24. |
| | **18** Create homemade gifts for people in your household using recycled items. | **19** Make paper snowflakes to give to neighbors. | **20** |
| | **25** | **26** | **27** |

# The Shepherds' Journey

Help the Shepherds get to baby Jesus.

# Christmas Jokes

**What kind of math is best to do before Christmas?**
Add-vent

**Why was Advent the restaurant worker's favorite season?**
Because she was a good waiter

**What was the Advent candle's favorite playground game?**
Hope-scotch

**Why is the candle of joy a different color?**
Because it was tickled pink

**Which Advent candle loves to eat green vegetables?**
The candle of peas

**Did you hear about the feeding trough that got a promotion?**
Now it's the assistant manger

**Why do people want to be guests at angels' homes?**
Because they are heavenly hosts

**What do you use to drain the pasta you eat in December?**
An Advent colander

**What kind of Christmas flower can show you the way?**
Point-settas

# Christmas Comic Strip

Look at the pictures and add your own words to create a Christmas comic. You can also use the next page to make your own Christmas comic strip. What part of the Advent story is your favorite?

© 2025 Cokesbury
ART: Naoko Matsunaga/Illustration Online LLC

# Create Your Own Comic

# Homemade Hot Cocoa

There is nothing better than a warm cup of hot cocoa at Christmastime. Enjoy this with your favorite Christmas cookie or snack.

*Recipe*

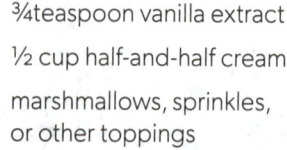

## Ingredients

¾ cup white sugar

½ cup unsweetened cocoa powder

1 pinch of salt

⅓ cup boiling water

3 ½ cups milk

¾ teaspoon vanilla extract

½ cup half-and-half cream

marshmallows, sprinkles, or other toppings

1. Combine the sugar, cocoa powder, and salt in a large saucepan and stir together.
2. Put the pan on the stove and carefully add in the boiling water. Have a grown-up help you!
3. Turn the stove to medium-high heat and let the cocoa come to a simmer and you see small bubbles.
4. Simmer and stir constantly for two minutes.
5. Turn off the stove and remove the pan from the heat. Pour in the milk and vanilla and stir some more.
6. Get your mugs and add a small amount of cream to each mug. Then pour the hot cocoa evenly into the mugs.
7. Add your toppings and enjoy!

Makes 4 servings

© 2025 Cokesbury
ART: Naoko Matsunaga/Illustration Online LLC, Adobe Stock

# Ornament Connect-the-Dots

Connect the dots to complete the ornaments and color the designs. Then add your own designs and colors.

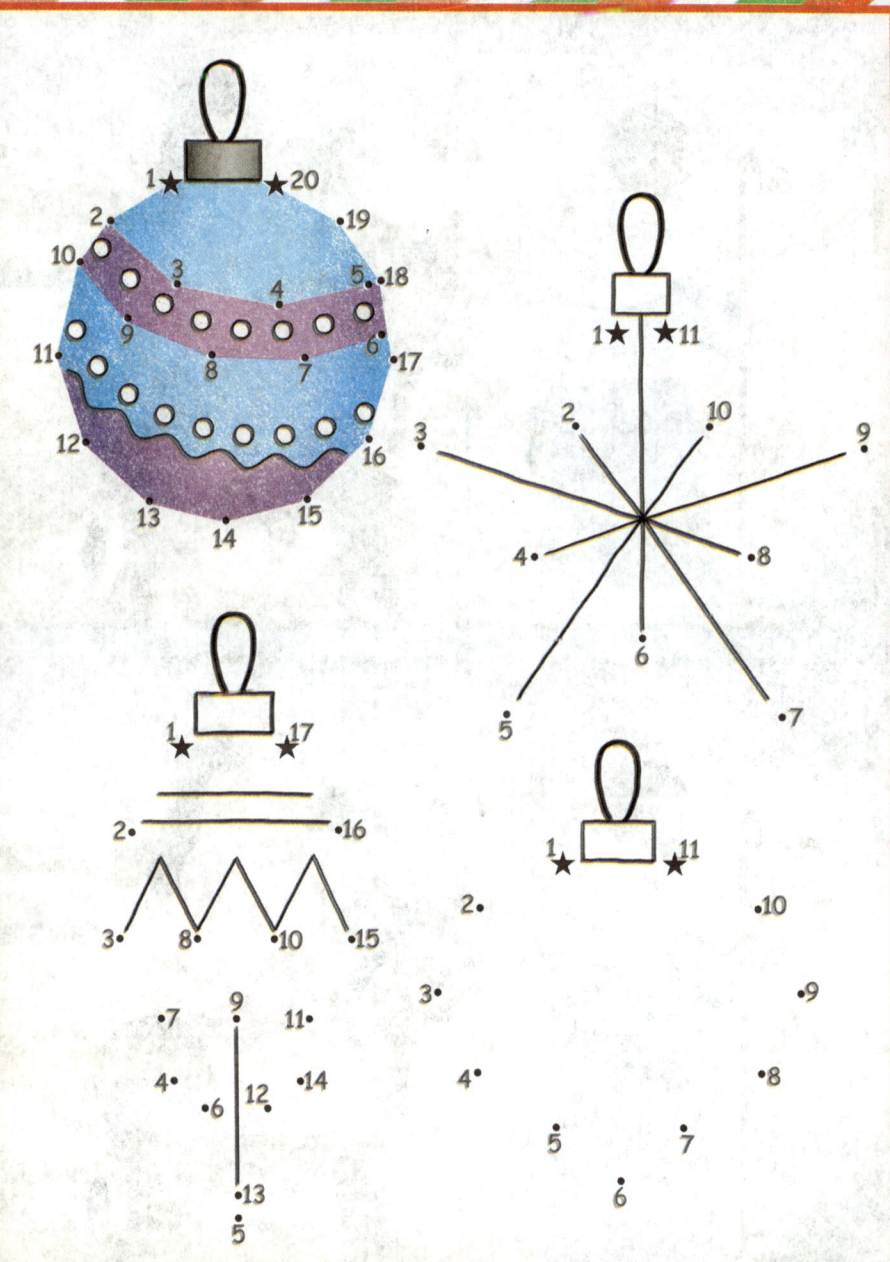

# Spot the Differences
Can you find the differences between the two pictures?

# Mindful Coloring

Find a quiet place to color and put on music or videos that help you feel calm. Use colors that remind you of Christmas or Advent. As you color, say a special prayer for what you hope for this Advent.

# Prayers for Advent

Use these prayers when you pray during Advent.

## A Prayer for Festivities and Fun:

God, even though it is dark outside, we see your light all over. We feel hope when the season changes and the decorations get put up. We feel peace during cozy times together. We feel joy because there are so many reminders of your promises. We feel love when we gather together. Help us spread your love to others.

## A Prayer before Drinking Hot Cocoa:

Lord, we know you created this good world. Thank you for these special moments. Fill us with joy that we can share with everyone. Amen.

## A Prayer for Singing Favorite Songs:

Thank you God for music making. Thank you for celebrations. Hear our praises. Help us feel you near. Amen.

## Breath Prayer:

(breathe in) I love you, Lord.

(breathe out) Help me love others.

## Body Prayer:

God, we wait for you today.

Help us share

hope (put hands out in front of you)

peace (show the two finger peace sign)

joy (do a dance)

and love (make fingers into a heart)

today. Amen.

## Prayer Walk:

Go with a grown-up on a walk, inside or outside, to look for symbols of the Advent and Christmas season. Pray each time you see one by simply saying: Thank you, God.

### When and where do you pray?

© 2025 Cokesbury
ART: Naoko Matsunaga/Illustration Online LLC, Adobe Stock

# Advent Prayer Journal

Write your own special prayers for Advent.

# Finger Prayer Labyrinth

Move your finger through the labyrinth as you pray or think about all the you have learned this Advent.